Sucker for Love

The Book

Cover Design: © 2013BrandDave

Published and distributed by

Possibilities Publishing Company
PO Box 10671
Burke, VA 22009
571-354-7386
www.possibilitiespublishingcompany.com

Contents:

Table of Contents

Forward

By Stephanie Garibaldi

Most people who know me well assume that I started directing a Valentine's Day storytelling show in 2009 to escape the horrible pressure, utter dismay, and ultimate discouragement that result from *never* having a date on Valentine's Day every year, year after year, and yes I mean NEVER.

Those people would not be wrong.

But that was not the only reason--just the glaringly obvious, primary one that got me started in 2009.

The other reason, which I swear also occurred to me at the time, is that the topic of love, romance, lust, or infatuation, whether you're dating, married, divorced, or anywhere in between, is so rich with possibilities. I mean, everyone ought to have at least one great story that falls within those wonderfully wide parameters, right? So it would be easy to cast the show—much easier than if the subject were say, people who get romantically involved with prisoners on death row. (Not that there's anything wrong with that; it's just a much narrower field.)

You cynical types out there are probably thinking that my primary motivators were the two big Ls: Loserhood and Laziness, but I prefer to think of them as the two big As: Availability and Accessibility. Hey, that's my story and I'm stickin' to it.

Whatever the motivation, I had it, and I was off and running with a call for online story submissions for SpeakeasyDC's yet untitled Valentine's Day show. When the audition dust cleared, I'd cast 9 brave souls with a wild mix of stories. None of us really knew what we were doing--least of all me, but we carried on as if we did, trusting the process, and somehow, it all wound up coming together. We rehearsed A LOT, so there was plenty of ensemble bonding. Everyone was incredibly supportive and encouraging of each other, as I'd direct them to be as open, intimate, and vulnerable as possible in their stories, without crossing over into that scary "boy-do-I-need-therapy" territory.

Somewhere amidst all those rehearsals, "Sucker for Love" was thrown out as a possible name for the show, and I jumped on it. Most titles have to grow on you, but this one just felt oh-so-right right off the bat.

The Sucker For Love show debuted in February 2009 in a small bar called Chief Ike's Mambo Room in the Adams Morgan neighborhood of DC. The first two shows sold out so quickly, that we ended up adding a third, which quickly became standing room only. We actually had people fighting over tickets in a way I haven't seen since the original, smaller stadium days of the Redskins' games—it was GLORIOUS!

I admit, I hadn't anticipated such rave reviews from critics and audience members alike. We hit on something more powerful than I'd dared to dream.

It turns out that while each story performed on our Sucker for Love stage and therefore each story featured in this Sucker for Love book is unique, it also has a highly relatable, universal appeal.

You'll find that this book contains something for everyone, just like our shows. No, really - It's true! If you're miserable on Valentine's Day and simply hate the holiday, we guarantee you'll read at least one story where the writer gets done so wrong that you'll feel better about your own lot in love. And no, it doesn't matter if you're male or female; if you're gay or straight; if you're married, divorced, or just so single it hurts; you will find stories you can relate to. Plus, there's always at least one story where love miraculously does somehow work out, giving hope to all of us suckers for love.

That is ultimately why I continue to love directing this show, year after year: for its universal appeal and for the hope it inspires in us hopeless types everywhere.

That is also why I was so thrilled to learn that a selection of Sucker for Love stories were being published as a book. It's wonderful to know that these compelling stories will have the chance to reach new audiences, or to be experienced by the same audiences in a new way. Plus, since SpeakeasyDC is a non-profit arts organization, proceeds from this book act as a fundraiser for the organization, which means that this book's sales will help us continue to put more great stories out into the world.

While this anthology could only feature 10 of the 38

Sucker for Love stories performed over the last four years, we hope it is the first of many annual Sucker for Love publications to come!

Here's what you'll get in this inaugural Sucker for Love anthology:

Twain Dooley still gets burned in spite of wooing with his brilliant spoken word poetry. Twain is an award-winning slam poet, and boy does it show even in his written pieces. He possesses that wonderful economy of words and interesting word combinations that serve him well live on stage or in print.

Anne Thomas shares a hilarious and touching tale about how she handles the unbridled love of a much younger man. Anne has that kind of subtle brilliance that sneaks up on you and startles you through her sly observations, keen wit, and emotional reactions woven between lines of dialogue. She is a passionate student of storytelling who has really come into her own savvy, sassy style.

Chris Love shares his heartbreaking-yet-comical tale of trying to "pack away the gay" and make sense of the crush he has on his best friend. Chris Love is a natural-born storyteller with a laid-back style all his own. He's comfortable talking about rather controversial topics in his honest, unflinching way. His stories are rich with detail and unexpected reactions.

Jessica Piscitelli Robinson takes a wry, unflinching look into the perilous world of dating when you're over 30, complete with bellies that tick, and hearts that don't always pound. Jessica Piscitelli is the PR powerhouse and fearless creative force behind both the videography business Capture Video Inc and storytelling organization Better Said Than Done. She's a published writer as well, as you'll see in her clean prose.

John Tong shares his usually-difficult-but-always-funny journey of trying to get it right with his girlfriend of 5 years. John is a gifted writer who came to SpeakeasyDC as a virgin storyteller, though you'd never guess it. His stories can surprise you with the unexpected tender moment that catches you off-guard, or the kind of moments that make you wonder what he could have possibly been thinking. Either way, they're as heartfelt as they are hilarious. John can make words dance and sing.

Travis Wright tries to follow his local pastor's advice to get a nice girlfriend and be a good man to her, in spite of just wanting to breed prize-winning dogs with his best friend. Travis is so down-to-earth funny that you'd probably never guess he has a doctorate degree in human development and psychology plus a master's degree in mental health counseling, both from Harvard-YOWSA! He shares his stories effortlessly, and he's always so relatable, no matter how unusual his subject.

Meredith Maslich shares the thrill of finding love that lasts past Saturday night, but what happens when she has to bring her man home to meet her family for the first time in her life? Meredith is a storytelling teacher and corporate trainer, so the woman knows how to structure a story and work a plot point for humor and punch. She'll let you see things as you've never seen them before, through her own vulnerable, insightful eyes.

Jeffrey Brady shares the funny and bizarre results when he moves to DC after finding a man as sophisticated and literary as himself. Jeffrey has the most delightful, quirky sense of humor running through all of his stories. While many of his stories tell of worldly adventures, his shining personality can make even the more mundane subjects exciting.

Nevin Martell falls so hard that he plots to propose big-movie style. Nevin is an incredibly talented writer who came to SpeakeasyDC to give performing live a shot. His Sucker for Love story was the first one he'd ever done for us, though in spite of being a storytelling virgin, you'll see that his eye for detail and sweet turn-of-phrase serve him well.

Vijai Nathan shares her the wild, awful, and unexpected places that online dating take this naive-but-brilliant comedian. Vijai is a wildly talented performer, as a journalist-turned-comedian-and-storyteller. She's written and performed 3 solo shows, plus taught others how to do the same through her SpeakeasyDC workshops and classes. Her story featured in this book will give you a mere taste of her riotous, take-you-by-surprise humor.

Redline Sucker

By Twain Dooley

I've always liked my women a little bit crazy. I can't be the only fool suffering from this affliction so I can't understand why no pharmaceutical company has conjured up a cure just yet.

The first time I see her is when she brushes by my shoulder and down the escalator to the red line. It's a hot, summer afternoon. She's wearing a brown mini-skirt and a frown. We end up on the same subway car. She's seated, I'm standing, pretending not to stare. I figure any woman that looks like she does – curly hair to her shoulders, thighs like café mocha—must've had fifteen-thousand men try to talk to her between work and the train. I didn't want to be fifteen-thousand and one. So I say nothing.

After a few stops, she rips off a piece of paper and takes out a pen. I'm intrigued. Is she writing a poem? A story idea? A letter to her senator? I want to ask but my stop is here so I move to get off. Just then, she looks at me and holds the paper in the air. It's her phone number. She hands it to me through the closing subway door and whispers one word, "Angie". If I weren't there I wouldn't believe it myself. This sort of thing only happens in the movies!

I grew up in Washington, DC where the women have always outnumbered the men so I never got in the habit of pursuit. Besides, chasing tail only makes one dizzy so I make up my mind: no matter how fine Angie is I'm not calling her… until the next day. When I do call, I only get her answering machine. I'm almost smooth, "Hello, um, Angie, um we met? On the subway, um. Give me a call?"

She doesn't call back.

I try again. I get her machine again. The outgoing message is her voice in a room with a slight echo and the splish of water. My imagination does back-over flips. I leave a message, "Wow, Angie. I'm really digging your answering machine and I would love to get to know the woman who created it. Give me a call, please."

She doesn't call back.

Maybe she regrets giving her number to a complete stranger. Maybe I shouldn't get frustrated just yet. Maybe I should just give it one more try, "Look here, Angie, you are one difficult woman to get in contact with. How about you let me know when's a good time to call you back."

She doesn't call back.

What kind of sick game is she playing? Maybe she's sitting there with a latte, listening to the shenanigans on her answering machine, twisting her curly locks. Maybe everybody on the subway has her phone number. She has problems. If she doesn't call me back, I'm never calling her ever again. Except this once.

This time I leave a cheesy little poem on her machine:

It's been seven days since

I wondered why an angel would ride

The subway instead of using her wings.

Seven days.

Longer than God took to create everything beautiful

One week and all can think is

"Angie"

She calls me back bubbling over like Alka-Seltzer. "I played your poem for all my friends! You are the most talented poet since Author Prysock." It turns out that not only does she like poetry but she likes Prince and I like Prince. Plus, she likes jazz and I pretend I like jazz. Of all the cars on all the subways in all the world, she was on mine. I never believed in fate until just then.

After about four hundred years, we go on our first evening date. I remember it well. I'm hiding from the rain under an awning, watching people dash by with Christmas presents in their clutches. Every clock, every watch anywhere nearby is running at least an hour fast. I know I'm in the right place and at the right time; that's all I've been able to think about since we decided to meet. She never shows. She never calls to say why she didn't show. I don't need this. I've got options. I resolve to never call her again.

I show up at her house. She claims that some fellow that she knows says he knows me—biblically. Who is this character? Why would he make up such kimchi? Is it her who is inventing, and why would she do that? Can I really account for every time I've had too much to drink? "Look", I tell her, "I'm straight, I want you, and if you want me too you won't make me play games." We kiss.

We play this extended game of phone tag for weeks or maybe months. I must be losing, I don't even know how to keep score. She leaves all sorts of madness on my answering machine, "Do you ever wonder what I feel like?" "I had my first marriage annulled. He called me a 'frigid bitch' just because I refused to have sex with him." She apparently has more baggage than I can carry. For the sake of my own sanity I decide to never call her again.

I show up at her job. She's wearing this long, velvety dress that's drizzled over her like a candy bar commercial. I take her back to my house where she kneels on my wall-to-wall pink carpet and fondles my cassette tape collection. I lay her down on my red futon and take photos of her. This is before she changes into a pair of my shorts, the smallest pair I could find. We make some Cuba Libre's, heavy on the Cuba and play strip tunk (She claims I used marked cards). The next morning when I take her home and she kisses me goodbye I feel like my patience has finally paid off. The world is a beautiful place. Nothing can break me down. Not even my car being broken into and my camera stolen. When I tell Angie about the car thing she asks, "You mean there is somebody out there masturbating to my pictures?" I guess so if thieves bother to develop film.

Did you ever have to scratch somebody out of your phonebook? Delete them from your phone? Have you ever been happy to find someone's number is not listed? The last time I saw her she was getting off the green line and I was getting on. She introduced the guy she was with as her boyfriend. I didn't know if I should feel jealous of the guy or sorry for him. She bubbles, "Oh my god, this is Twain Dooley. This is the poet I've been telling you about. Oh, Twain, I miss you so much."

I've always liked my women a little bit crazy. Sensible women, practical ones, the type who always match their panties and bras bore me a little too easily. It took me a while to admit that to myself. Once I did, I found the type of madness I can deal with. And I no longer take phone numbers from strangers on the subway.

Cougar in a Wheelchair

By Anne Thomas

I am on a plane from London to Cairo to begin a romance in the flesh that blossomed over the internet. I met Mourad six months ago when I was touring in Egypt. He was my tour guide and we had a great, fun connection. When I left the country, he gave me the biggest bouquet of flowers I have ever seen this side of the Miss America pageant; two dozen white carnations ringed by passionate red roses. And when I landed at Dulles airport and checked my emails, there was one from him saying that he missed me. And so the romance began. The thing is though, I am 50 and he is 22!

So I'm out of my mind right?! This can never work. The age difference is too great. He is geographically undesirable in the extreme. He's very religious, I am not. And yet, I am drawn to him. He texts me pictures made with cell phone symbols of hearts and sends me short sweet poems like:

Lives are for living I live for you
Dreams are for dreaming I dream for you
Hearts are for beating mine beats for you
Angels are for keeping. Can I keep you?

Who can resist that, right? I can't, even though I know I am courting societal disapproval by pursuing this romance. At least I'm giving people something juicy to talk about.

The plane lands and as I clear customs and go out into the crowded reception area, my stomach is in knots. I am so nervous I could puke. I think about our age difference; about the text messages and phone calls that form the slim basis of my taking this long trip to see him again and I worry about my attractiveness; not just because of my age, but the fact that I use a wheelchair too.

I search for Mourad in the crowd, and when I get to the end of the gated area, I see him. He is medium in height with brown eyes, a classic Arabic nose and short wavy hair shaved high on the sides and slicked back on top. He looks nervous too, which I find comforting. He greets me chastely with a kiss on the cheek and says, "Anne, Welcome back to Cairo."

"Mourad, I'm so happy to see you again."

He turns from me and says, "Anne, this is Moustafa our driver, and my friend Mahmood." I had not counted on a welcoming committee! This just adds to my nervousness. But of course, he is only 22 and does not own or know how to drive a car, so I should have expected this.

Mourad and I sit in the back seat of the car together. We are in a Muslim country so we cannot touch. But my coat is on the seat between us and he seeks out my hand under cover of my coat. I feel like I am in High School. It is awkward and sweet and I am on the verge of hysterical laughter at the situation.

Mourad tells me, "My father is not well."

"I'm sorry to hear that. Do they know what is wrong?"

"Something with his liver."

"How old is he?"

"He is very young, only 58."   I physically choke at the closeness of his father's age to mine and now I have to know his mother's age.

"And how old is your mother?"

"She too is very young. Only 52." I am only two years younger than his mother! I am going to have that hysterical outburst now!

We get to the hotel, and as soon as the bellman leaves us alone in my room, Mourad is on top of me, kissing me, hard, fast, excited and with far more passion than skill.

He says, "You know I have never kissed a woman before." Oh dear God! I thought he probably was a virgin being a devout Muslim, but never kissed anyone either?! Now I totally feel like a Cougar! A Cougar in a wheelchair!

"That's okay Mourad. It just makes our being together that much more special."
His eyes glance down and he says, softly, "Habibi, you

know, I cannot make love to you. It is forbidden in Islam. Even kissing you is wrong outside of marriage," and then his eyes meet mine again, and this time his voice is filled with longing "but I **must** kiss you."

I smile, "That's okay Sweetheart. We don't have to make love. It is probably better that we don't." In fact, I am relieved. Things are moving fast enough as it is.

Still looking me in my eyes, he says, "I love you Anne. I told myself for a while that I just liked you, but that is not true. I am sure I love you."

I am surprised and flummoxed by his declaration. "Mourad, isn't it a little too soon to be talking about love?"

With great sincerity he says, "No. In Egypt, our parents find us girls who are from good families, beautiful and kind. We meet them and then we know if we can love them. My brothers only met their wives one or two times before they married and they love them."

I have to make him understand how differently Americans approach marriage. "Yes, but in my country we have to sleep with you and live with you for a couple of years before we can decide if we love you or not!" And I laugh to myself when I say that because it sounds so absurd.

He smiles. "Anne, I know I love you. I know you are beautiful and kind and I can tell you come from a good family. Don't you love me?" I don't know if I love him. I barely know him at all, so to avoid the question all together, I distract him with kisses.

Later he pulls back and says, "Oh my God, there are red marks all over your neck." I rush to the mirror. He gave me hickeys! I am 50 years old and my neck is covered in hickeys! I immediately wonder when the lobby shops will open the next day so I can buy a scarf to hide my Western whorish neck.

After I get my scarf, Mourad takes me to a pretty park on a hill. It is a couples park. Couples sit together on benches, some hold hands, some quietly talk. The average age is about 20. I am torn between hysterical laughter again and being moved that Mourad has brought me here because I am his girl.

That evening as I am instructing him further in the ways of amour, Mourad grandly asks me, "If... If, I asked you to marry me, what would you say?"

I am stunned by this question and stall for time. "Ahhhhhhh, that's a really big question. I have a lot of questions before I can answer a question like that."

"What are your questions?"

"Well, where would we live?"

"Cairo!" he says with great pride and ownership in the place. I am surprised and glad. I was afraid he was going to say the US and confirm my friend's suspicions that he is pursuing me in hopes of getting into my country.

I position myself to look Mourad directly face to face. "Don't you think I'm too old for you? I'm working towards the end of the life cycle and you are just beginning yours. I am just going to get more wrinkly with white hair and you will still be young and beautiful."

"No," he says emphatically, "age makes no difference. You will always be beautiful Anne on the inside."

For a moment, I think he has forgotten how old I am. I look at him deeply and tenderly, "Mourad, I am too old to have children."

He softly says, "I know."

I am so touched by his words. They are earnest, and words all women want to hear, but I came here as a lark, an adventure, to live fully, not to get married.

"Mourad, it's not so simple. I have significant health problems." I am desperately trying to dissuade him from wanting to marry me. It is too much, too soon. With emphasis, Mourad says, "Anne, you do not understand how much I love you. I don't care about your health problems. I want to be with you and take care of you for the rest of my life. Do you agree to marry me?"

I am trying to push him away and he offers me such

beauty. He offers me unconditional love. But he is young and idealistic and I am old and too cynical to believe or receive that his love is real or could last.

"Mourad, I cannot live in Egypt. It would be too hard for me. What if they don't let you into my country."

Softly, Mourad says "Anne, I love you. If I only saw you one or two weeks of the year, that would be enough.

"Mourad, that is not enough for me."

"Then I will come to your country. We will try to get a visa for me."

The US government did not grant him a visa, and the relationship petered out after a couple of years. But in the end, I'm not sure if I was out of my mind more for beginning this May/December romance or for letting it go.

First Kiss

By Christopher Love

I knew years before my first nocturnal emission that I was gay. Which was quite a burden for an 11-year-old growing up in early 80s, Corn Belt Ohio. My feelings for a shirtless, sparring Tony Danza on *Taxi* were confusing. The AIDS hysteria plaguing the country was frightening. So I willfully packed away the gay. I figured I could acknowledge my feelings to myself, but to no one else. At least until I could leave the town my social studies teacher called Corn Junction.

This strategy works for years. Until my belated puberty coincides with getting my driver's license and meeting Dave Sadowski. Everyone in my town is from here, except for a few people from such exotic places as Akron. Or Pittsburgh. That's Dave -- from Pittsburgh. And in a Sears Roebuck - JC Penney town, the Sadowskis are an LL Bean family. They have plaid wallpaper *and* a matching tartan dog bed. Dave wears Duck Boots with the laces undone, plays piano for fun, and listens to the Mamas and the Papas, not Molly Hatchet and Iron Maiden like the rest of my town. He's the boy who first merges my names into one: *ChrisLove*. He can't speak a sentence to me without sighing my name, his face breaking into an intoxicating smirk. And he's a poet at heart. He puts his arm around me at school, "ChrisLove, watch how the snow dances in the wind. So beautiful." He watches the snow in awe as I watch him in awe as the boys around us fart in each other's faces.

We become fast friends. "ChrisLove, I want to play something beautiful for you", and he sits down at his piano and sings *Dream a Little Dream of Me*. And oh, how I do. He lies down next to me on the hunter green carpet in his living room. "ChrisLove, you know that feeling you get when you wake up in the middle of the night, no one's up, and it's so quiet and peaceful. That's what I hope death is like." This preppie poet-philosopher is killing me. As if that weren't enough, his diabetes often makes him a little loopy and even more irresistible. His posture escapes him and he leans into me like a golden retriever. "ChrisLove, will you give me my shot? You're the only one who does it right." He pulls up his shirt to expose his stomach for the injection. I melt. Let's face it, he had me at hyperglycemic shock.

One night, Dave steals beer from his dad. We race to the Scioto River, making his family's paneled station wagon fly over each of the seven hills. We walk along the shore. "ChrisLove, do you ever feel like you're going to be alone forever? I just want to kiss a girl. Oh, I love you, ChrisLove." As he kisses me on the cheek, he sinks into me. His diabetic delirium typically makes for some mixed messages. But I don't acknowledge to myself that Dave might be gay. As clear as the signs are, I'm developing the unique ability to read ambiguity into blatant overtures. Which is a less-than-helpful dating strategy I use to this day.

Eventually, Dave finds a girlfriend. "Oh ChrisLove,

we're going to find a girl for you. ChrisLove, kissing is so amazing and soft." I stoically listen to the reports of his first romance until I can escape home to the mixed tape he made for me. It's the Mixed Tape of Mixed Messages. And songs that have always been background music in my life take on new meaning. Marianne Faithfull, Roberta Flack, the Stones. The lyrics give voice to my feelings. I sit in my room pining for him, listening to the cassette over and over again. And *as tears go by, he's killing me softly,* and *my whole world turns black.*

But, even with a girlfriend, his affection for me doesn't change. His desire to get me drunk doesn't change. I still give him his shots. And touch his skin. "I love you ChrisLove. What would I do without you?"

Before leaving for college, I figure I have nothing to lose, so I come out to Dave and tell him about my feelings for him. He declares, *"I love my new gay ChrisLove,"* before slumping onto me. That summer, nothing really changes after I come out to him. Which is good. But, nothing really changes after I come out to him. Which isn't so good.

I leave Dave behind for his final year of high school. My first semester of college is not the transformative experience I'd hoped for. And I listen to Dave's mixed tape when I feel lonely. I listen to Dave's mixed tape a lot.

I head home for Christmas Break, and I'm between worlds. I spot Dave as he genuflects at Christmas Mass.

He's in his Duck Boots, red and black plaid jacket, and bomber hat. And the same feelings come rushing back. All I want to do is see him during my break, but all I do is avoid him. I finally agree to go to a New Year's party with him. It's hosted by this girl, Jeni, who dots her i with a smiley face. The soybean fields surrounding the house are lit up by a neon Jesus that shines through her window. Dave keeps calling me out to the hot tub, but I stay inside most of the night to avoid him and his girlfriend as they get drunker and drunker. Close to midnight, I give in to Dave … well, he threatens to drag me into the hot tub. I get in, stone sober, with Dave, his girlfriend, and the host Jeni who has changed into a bubblegum pink bikini to coordinate with her baby blue eye shadow and her over-bleached, over-permed hair. The moment I get in, Dave and his girlfriend start making out. Through the open door, the countdown begins:

10 – *Someone's flashing the neon Jesus on and off.*
9 - *Jeni's hand is on my thigh.*
8 - *The neon lights up her bubble-gum chest.*
7 - *Oh shit. Her hand's moving up my thigh.*
6 - *Dave's girlfriend pulls down his trunks.*
5 - *She mounts him.*
4 - *They're moaning.*
3 - *Oh shit, they're having sex.*
2 - *Jeni grabs my face.*
1 - *She jabs her tongue down my throat.*

It's 1988. And it's my first kiss.

Jeni stands and pumps her wine cooler into the air.

Dave and his girlfriend keep moaning. The snow swirls in the wind. I sit in the hot tub, paralyzed. I didn't choose to be a voyeur. Wait -- Dave kept calling me out here. Was this whole thing staged? Unnoticed tears flow down my face. I turn to get out. Dave grabs my arm. "Hey, you're my ride. Don't forget me ChrisLove." Forget? He's the boy who taught me beauty and pain. "Don't forget, I love you, ChrisLove."

I need to get him his shot.

The Game

By Jessica Piscitelli Robinson

I first met Roy at a networking event. Okay, it was a meetup. Okay it was a meetup for singles who like to drink, which, judging by appearances of all the people there meant old, overweight, and with no sense of style.

I was there with my friend Meredith and we had gone with the intention of finding and winning a couple of fine looking men. In this crowd though, it would be like shooting fish in a barrel. I am not the hottest thing this side of the Mississippi, but I can hold my own in a room full of circus freaks, and since that was exactly what we had walked into, we were the star attraction. It was disheartening.

And then, we saw it – across the room – a beacon of hope. Two guys standing together who were not Brad Pitt or Hugh Jackman, but they would do. They were wearing clothes made post 1970, could still see their toes past their bellies, and wouldn't remember where they were the day Kennedy was shot. We were in business. Like the only Democrats lost at a Republican conference, we gravitated towards each other and started talking.

Meredith got the one guy's number and I gave mine to Roy.

On our first date, when the waiter came by, I ordered a

cheeseburger, which surprised Roy. "You sure you want a cheeseburger? Not a salad?"

"Nope. I am in the mood for a cheeseburger." I smiled at the waiter and then Roy ordered a cheeseburger too, but couldn't let it go at that.

"You could've ordered something more expensive. Are you trying to be low maintenance or something? I mean, don't get me wrong, I'm not complaining, just wondering what your game is."

"I don't play games," I explained. "I just love a good burger."

As the night wrapped up, he asked me to guess how old he was, which was awkward. I am terrible with ages, and I didn't want to insult him. He looked like he was in his 40s, but I figured it would be safer to guess way below that, so I said "35?" He laughed and said, "No, really." So I said "39?" We played the guessing game a little longer, but he said he'd only give me the answer on our next date.

There was nothing wrong with our first date. I wasn't blown away, but I had fun, and he had fun, so we met for the second date. I got to learn how old he was – not yet 30. It's not my fault he looked like a well preserved forty year old instead of a not so in shape twenty something. We laughed about it, and moved on, and he was convinced that I had just been playing him.

Six months later, we were still dating. Just dating. It

was always fun. He was nice, made me laugh, made good money. Whenever we hung out with my family, my nieces called him Uncle Roy and he made them laugh and was great with them and then my belly started making this ticking noise and I remembered that I was over thirty.

We had the talk. I said, "We should be exclusive, or we should break up." He said, "I like my freedom." I said, "You never date anyone else. I'm the only one dating other people." He said, "I just want to keep my options open."

It was infuriating. I was the one with options, not him, but he didn't want to commit. I said, "Fine, let's break up." He thought that it was a joke, that I wasn't actually prepared to leave, but I don't play games. He didn't want to break up, so we stopped seeing other people.

There was nothing wrong with our relationship. We never fought. We had the same sense of humor. We got along great. Neither of us demanded much of the other person and I always had a date for the weekend. And then it was six months later and my belly was still ticking, even if my heart wasn't exactly pounding.

I was, let's be honest, better looking than him, even though he didn't know it. He still thought he had the same figure he had been sporting since college, without ever working out, but it wouldn't be long before he lost sight of his toes. I made him laugh and put up with his crappy hours at work, which included evening and weekend hours more often than not. And, as much as I enjoyed being taken out to dinner, I cooked him a lot of great homemade meals. It bugged me that he wasn't pushing for more of a commitment. I am a great catch! It felt like time for another talk.

I said, "We should move in together." He said, "I don't think I am ready." I said, "Well maybe we should break up then." He said, "You wouldn't leave me, you love me too much."

But I wasn't playing. I said "Fine, let's break up," so he said, "No, no, let's move in together." And that's when things changed.

It was like those scenes in Bugs Bunny when Bugs is arguing with Elmer Fudd. Elmer says "get in the cauldron." Bugs says "no." Elmer says "yes." Bugs say "no." Elmer says "yes." Bugs says "yes" and then Elmer's saying no and Bugs is saying yes and it's all flipped around.

As soon as Roy said, "Okay, let's move in together," I thought, "Oh shit, I don't want that." And then I was saying "No, no. We should take our time and think about it" but he had outplayed me.

"You can live with me and rent out your townhouse," he said. He was ready to do it. And there I was with this ticking belly but no pounding heart.

I had played at pushing him away and he had played at not being in love. It was my move. I told him we should break up, for real.

He still thought it was a game. He said, "Are you trying to protect me? Are you dying and don't want me to know?" I said "No, I'm not."

He said, "Where did this come from? Are you having a nervous breakdown?" I said "No, I'm not. I am sorry."

He came by a few days later, ostensibly to return my stuff. He asked me if we could go for a walk. We were walking in the woods behind my house when he stopped me and said, "You win." He held out a diamond ring and declared, "I am in love with you. I am sorry I made you wait, but I am ready to spend the rest of my life with you."

I started sobbing. This wasn't what I had wanted. Once I calmed down enough to talk, I said, "I can't marry you."

At first he thought it was a ploy, that I was angling for a better proposal. He said, "We don't have to count this as the proposal. You don't even have to say yes right now. We'll just get back together and then I'll surprise you. Later. But soon."

I had to convince him that I really meant it. "I can't marry you. I don't really love you."

It hurt to say it, but as realization dawned on him, I knew it hurt him a lot more. He backed away from me, like I was going to slap him, and said, "You are crazy."

We walked back to my house in silence. I could only imagine what he was feeling. For my part, I just felt guilt. Roy left me at the door and didn't come back and we were, finally, broken up, for real.

He had thought all along that I was playing him, and as he walked away, defeated, I realized I had been. I had been playing at making him love me, because I thought he should. And in the end, I won.

With This Promise Taco, I Thee Wed

By John Tong

I dated my wife for five years before proposing, which I have been told is a long time… repeatedly by my wife.

I am a cynical person and that makes me hard to love. For a long time I thought the most common marriage proposal was: *"YOU'RE WHAT?"*

I had no idea women have this "consensus" that the man should propose after dating a year or two. I knew I always wanted to marry Nicole, (my wife), but there was always something in the way. First we weren't living together, then she was in graduate school and then there were our families.

When we first started dating, I was living with my brother and that was an issue for Nicole. My brother is wildly inappropriate and doesn't understand "social cues." Before Nicole came over, I had to literally remind him that his shorts had to be longer than his penis.

Our first Christmas together, her sister sang "Felice Navidad" to me over the telephone. I was, like, "Why are you singing me this song?" And she said, "I'm sorry, I heard you were ethnic."

Our first Thanksgiving, work prevented Nicole from going home to visit her family. So I asked my mom if she could come to Thanksgiving. My mom takes the holidays very seriously, and I'm a gigantic momma's boy, so when she said "we hadn't dated long enough for her to consider it serious," I didn't put up much of a fight.

So, Nicole had Thanksgiving dinner by herself and, because Cracker Barrel was too expensive, she went to O'Charley's. Which is basically having Thanksgiving at a soup kitchen, but they bring you a bill at the end.

I wonder if that Thanksgiving meal gave her the strength she needed to get through the next four years. Surrounded by these desperately lonely bastards, eating warmed over sliced turkey, I think she had looked into the Abyss... and the Abyss looked back and showed her an image of me and went, "meh."

Meanwhile, her entire family was still adjusting to the prospect of incorporating a large, sensitive Chinese man into their family. Her father, Mike, is a retired Marine Master Sargent. Mike dislikes things like taxes and the homosexual agenda.

I will tell you one story about my relationship with Mike. One Christmas before we were married, Nicole went to her hometown Harley Davidson store to get her father a gift.

The clerk behind the counter recognized her name and asked in a slack-jawed drawl,

"Are you one of Mike Foreman's girls?"

She said, "yes."

"Are you Jennifer, or the one dating the Chinese pussy?"

I viewed this as progress because at least Mike wasn't calling me a "pussy" to my face anymore.

II.

Although I am a cynic, I'm also a failed romantic. I try to create these grand romantic gestures and then watch as they completely disintegrate before my eyes.

One year, for Valentine's Day, I did that box-inside-a-box thing for my wife. I got a few presents. I put one of them in really big box and another in a smaller box inside that box and so on until there was this one really tiny box inside all the other boxes.

Now, I have been told that this is a very lame idea… repeatedly, by my wife. I never realized that this was a very clichéd way that some men propose marriage.

Inside one of the boxes was a Russian, nesting, Matryoshka doll that I encouraged her to open. And after opening each one she discovered they were devoid of any jewelry whatsoever.

I said, "see, it's a *doll-inside-a-doll* inside a *box-inside-a-box*."

That was the conceptual innovation I was bringing to

the table. And I knew I had done a good job because of how hard she was crying. And rather than justifiably leaving me at that very moment, she foolishly opened the last and smallest box and inside she found... a gift certificate to my favorite Mexican restaurant or, as I like to think of it, a "promise taco".

I am sure she could tell you many, many more stories of how completely clueless I am regarding romantic acts. But as the years marched on, I sensed it was getting time to propose because every time we went to the mall Nicole would take me on this continuous loop of the jewelry stores.

So I started going ring shopping to poke my toes in the water. I went by myself which was a mistake.

See, when a couple goes ring-shopping together they are searching for a token of their love that she can cherish forever. But when a man goes ring shopping alone, he negotiates with a stranger to determine the cash-valuation of his significant other. It's like arriving at a price for sex with a hooker that lived through the Depression.

I went to a local, fancy jewelry store first. I was greeted at the front door by a gorgeous, young woman in, like, an evening gown. Her name was Candy. I told her I was looking for a diamond engagement ring and she escorted me to a special, marbled area.

The salesman oozed over to me.

"Hey, I hear you're looking for an engagement ring. How many carats are you looking for?"

I said, earnestly, "Well, the internet says that I should be more concerned with clarity."

"Sure it does," he said patronizingly. "Let's just go ahead and look at some rings I picked out."

No ring was less than two carats or $20,000.

Balking, I said, "I don't know... My wife is really petite and, well, I think these rings might be too big for her."

"Too big? *Too big?* Candy!" He said as he motioned for her to come over.

"Candy, can it ever get... too big?" She immediately blushed and started giggling. "Oh no, of course not," she said with a wink.

Of course the first thought in my head was, "wow, Candy is a filthy whore." But then I realized that this guy was trying to make me feel inadequate so I would over compensate and buy a bigger ring. Of course, what all these salespeople didn't know was that I was highly attenuated to this particular sales technique because my entire life has been dominated by a vicious cycle of inadequacy and overcompensation. That's my wheelhouse.

So, I just stood up and left. This was not going to be a repeat of my gym membership.

III.

Despite my experiences buying the ring, I did find myself getting more and more into finding the ring. And as a byproduct, more and more excited about the prospect of actually proposing.

The year I proposed, Nicole spent the entire month of January at a writer's colony in Vermont. I came up with this grand plan that I would fly to Vermont, surprise her and propose to her in my hometown of Williamstown, Massachusetts. I hadn't set foot there for 15 years and in my mind I had idealized winter in New England. Frozen brooks, Birch trees, quietly snowing... ever since I left, that's how I remembered it.

I had no idea where in Williamstown to propose to Nicole, so I asked my brother if he had any ideas. He immediately suggested that I propose at the foot of our father's grave. I wasn't sure if I wanted to go Goth with the whole thing, so I told him that'd be my "Plan B."

So, without a spot picked out, I flew up to Vermont. When I got there, Nicole was completely surprised to see me. Better yet, she had no idea what I was planning due to the aforementioned five years of crushing disappointment.

I told her that I was going to drive her down to Williamstown to visit an art museum. What I didn't tell her was I was going to propose to her behind the museum on this huge stone bench I remembered from my childhood.

We drive to the museum. I'm nervous, but not too nervous. Let's face it: she's five years in at this point... I'm basically a junk bond she's over leveraged... she is so upside down in this relationship, she has to say "yes."

After we look at art, I ask her if she wants to go for a walk. So we trudge up this hill, in two feet of snow and it's -17 degrees outside. When we got to the bench and I saw how small it actually was, I realized that either I was much, much smaller as a child or my ass had unfurled itself like a flower in a Georgia O'Keefe painting.

So, now I'm nervous.

I didn't have any place to propose, so I'm trying to figure this out on the fly. I drove her to a wonderful vista I remembered from my childhood - now there were condos. We drove to the first house we lived in, where my father had planted a beautiful garden – now it's a parking lot.

On the outside, I was trying to stay cool, but in my head I was freaking out. We went to every corner of that town and I was sweating in my heavy coat; I smelled like Nell Carter after a camping trip. Then, in desperation, I remembered one last place.

So, as we were standing over my father's grave... it dawns on me that this probably isn't a good idea.

So we started to leave town. And as we were leaving we

passed a little forest I grew up next to. I told her I wanted to go on another hike, and she was like, "*another one?*" I said I wanted to look around for a minute. So we walked into the forest. I saw this moss-covered rock off to the side of the trail and told her I wanted to sit down.

We trudged into the snow, sat on the rock.

Then, I noticed the rock was overlooking a ravine… with a frozen brook… surrounded by birch trees… it was absolutely silent and we were completely alone and, at that very moment, it started to softly snow.

She snuggled closer to me and said, "this has been the best day of my entire life."

That instant, that moment will always remain one of my most cherished memories. It's like a photograph I will never get tired of looking at. To this day, it amazes me that someone so beautiful and smart would be such a sucker to marry a guy like me.

We recently celebrated the six year anniversary of that day and we've been married for five years now. But if you ask my wife, she'll tell you, she deserves credit for all eleven.

Best in Show
By Travis Wright

When Patrick said, "I like Belgian Sheepdogs," I felt the hair on my arms stand-up. It was the summer after 6th grade and he was a participant in the "Dog Care and Training" workshop I was leading at 4H camp.

Shocked and intrigued, I asked him, "Why do you like Belgians?" Without hesitation, he responded, "They are bold and handsome. I want to show them." It was like all of the air had just been sucked out of the room—I looked right at him and it was like no one else was in the world. To this day, twenty-something years later, I can still remember that first moment that I "saw" him.

You see, I, too, loved Belgian Sheepdogs. I had never met another person who even knew what they were. I spent hours looking at pictures of them in my World Book Encyclopedia. Even though I had never seen one in person, I dreamed about winning Best in Show at the Westminster Kennel Club dog show someday with my very own handsome Black Belgian Stud. I fantasized about running around that big ring in the Center of Madison Square Garden—dressed in my tuxedo and everyone clapping for me. The judge, a sophisticated elder woman dressed in sparkling sequins slowly raising her hand, pointing at me, and saying, "Best in Show."

It was like something inside me just knew that Patrick understood this dream, this deep part of me. I have since heard people talk about split-a-parts—one soul, split in two, and then sent to roam the world looking for its other half. These two parts coming back together explains the "click" that some people feel when they fall in love. In this moment at the Clyde Austin 4H training Center, Patrick and I clicked. But, I was in 6th grade. What did I know at the time? Unschooled in the ways of romance, and indoctrinated in the ways of the Southern Baptist Church, there was no way that I could have known the true nature of my feelings.

Nevertheless, I was thrilled to discover that Patrick and I would be attending the same school at the end of the summer, and that he lived not too far from my family. We would be able to continue our friendship. For the rest of July and August we spent hours roaming the woods behind my house, talking about Dallas and Falcon Crest, and discussing which other purebred dog breeds we would most like to show. I felt like I could always be myself with Patrick.

But just as Danny Zuko and Sandra Dee discovered in Grease, real life and summer vacation are not the same. As the school year approached, the expectations of real life began to intrude. On the Sunday eve before the beginning of my 7th grade school year, our preacher pulled all of the seventh and 8th grade boys into a room at church and said, "Fellas. It is time to start growing up. I want you boys to become real men."

Brian Baskette raised his hand and said, "What do you mean, real men?"

Pastor White responded, "A real man takes care of all of the women in his life. He marries a good woman, is a good father to his daughter, and makes sure to always honor and respect his mother. It is time for you to start practicing, spending more time with girls, playing less freeze tag. Maybe you should even get a little girlfriend."

That sounded fine to me, the only problem was that the idea of kissing girls or holding their hands made me slightly nauseous. Don't get me wrong, I loved girls—talking with them, playing with them, sharing Easy Bake oven recipes. It was just that whole seeing them naked thing that didn't melt my butter.

I wondered, "Why couldn't it be as easy as hanging out with Patrick or the other boys?" I didn't mind seeing them naked. After all, I was the king of Truth or Dare in my Cub Scout troop. Everyone knew that they couldn't come into my tent at Cub Scout camp unless they took their clothes off. And, everyone wanted to come to my tent. We would hang out for hours laughing, talking, thumb wrestling.

So freaked out was I by the new "Real Man Initiative" that I one day found Preacher White before Sunday school and asked, "Why must boys and girls get married?" He said simply that it was God's plan. I said to him, "But what if it makes you nervous? Does God want me to feel sick?" He laughed and said, "We all feel that way. Marriage is hard. Sometimes you don't like each other very much. But you have to work at it." He patted me on the head and said, "God has made the perfect woman just for you. You just have to look for her." Maybe that was it. I just hadn't been looking hard enough. I decided I would start.

The next morning on the school bus, I related the details of the conversation to Patrick. He seemed slightly perturbed, but said that if I felt I must pursue this church real man-thing, he understood. But, he warned me that dating would take time away from our dog show dreaming. I told him that I didn't want that either, but that I had to do this. I would do my best not to let it interfere. Before pulling out the most recent issue of Dog Fancy, Patrick ended the conversation by saying, "Well, just be careful what you get a hold of. These girls can be a hand-full."

For efficiency's sake, I decided a needed a strategy. All the boys at school seemed to really like the cheerleaders, so I figured that maybe I would be a real man for one of them. I made a note for each member of the squad, "Will you go with me, check yes or no." I passed them around during lunch and waited for the replies. I was thrilled when Tasha Gray passed hers back to me with a big heart on the front and a check in her yes box. Ok, I thought, this is good. I'm going to be a real man to her. I gave her my ice cream money at lunch, showed her my math homework, and even packed her a sensible snack for our field trip. Mom was so proud that I had a girlfriend.

I thought she was a real lady—that is, until the bus ride home from our school visit to the local poultry processing plant.

One of the kids was saying how bad the place smelled. We were all laughing that it smelled like a cross between puke and poop. That's when Tasha yelled, "I bet it didn't smell as bad as this!" And then she let out the most enormous bun shaker you have ever heard. And it was disgusting!

I was absolutely mortified. How could my little lady be such a truck driver? Before he left, my dad farted all the time and my mom would always say, "No man loves his family if he is willing to punish them like that." And she was right. I hated living my with dad's gas—and there was no way I was going to live with Tasha's. That's why, as soon as the bus pulled back onto campus, I looked at her and said, "I can't do this anymore. This just isn't working for me." I knew I had made the right decision when she burped in my face and said, "If you can't stand the heat, get out of the kitchen." Right then and there, I realized that dating red neck pre-teens in east Tennessee was not going to be easy.

Dejected, I was sitting slumped over on the school bus later that afternoon when Patrick slid into the seat with me. When he asked me what was wrong, I said that I was having my first broken heart, and explained that things had gone south with Tasha. When I explained to him what happened, he smiled and said, "You have to watch those blondes. They will break your heart every time."

Hmmm…maybe that was it. Just like preacher White had said, I picked the wrong one. That's why the next day, I asked Stephanie, the only red head in school, if she would like to go with me. A member of the basketball team, a little taller than me, and sexy in that Ms. Jane Hathaway kind of way, she was everything that my little cheerleader wasn't. I was thrilled when she said yes. I was especially happy when she said that she would only do it if it didn't mean any of that hand holding stuff. And things were great until a few days later at recess. I was keeping score for her as she shot lay ups, when one of the rowdy boys ran by and said, "Hey Ginger, does the carpet match the drapes?" Before I could stand up to defend my woman's honor, Stephanie grabbed her crotch and shouted, "Red on the head, fire in the hole."

I am not exactly sure I understood what she meant, but it definitely didn't seem lady like. And, it was clear that Stephanie didn't need me to take care of her. I mean, how could I be a real man to someone who was, well, a little more manly than me?

Eventually, I came clean to Patrick about my challenges with girls. During a 7th grade sleepover, while we were lying next to each other in bed, I said to him, "Can I tell you something? A secret." He said, "Of course, you can tell me anything." "Ok, then," I said. "I am having a hard time with girls---- I'm just not sure I feel comfortable kissing them."

Patrick said, "Oh, I talked with my mom about that. I feel the same way. She said it was because I am a man of God. God has taken away my lustful heart until I get older, so that I won't get a girl pregnant or commit any really big sins or anything like that. She said that someday I would meet the right woman when I least expected it—she would just find me and snatch me up. God would see to that."

Hmmmm….. this really made sense to me. After my traumatic experiences with Tasha and Stephanie, I decided to take a break from dating for a while. I mean, all of this time with the girls was really cutting into my time with my best friend, Patrick. And, ironically, all of this time with girls was making me feel very, well, un-manly. I never felt this way when with Patrick.

Milestones
By Meredith Maslich

I'd been dating Chris for seven months when I decided to bring him home to meet my family. As we got into the car to make the seven hour drive from Fairfax, Virginia to Rochester, New York the rain was biblical in its intensity. I might have seen that as a bad sign, if I were the type of person to believe in signs. Which, as of that moment, I no longer was. Not only was this Chris's first time meeting my family, but it was also, at 35 years old, my first time bringing a boyfriend home. I had enough to worry about without trying to read into the weather.

Chris is the first guy I've ever dated long enough - or more to the point- functionally enough, to get to this milestone. From the first moment of our first date everything about the relationship was so easy, so fun, so too good to be true. And given my rocky 15 year dating history, I became more focused on the "too good to be true" part over the "so easy, so fun" part. If there was one thing I'd learned, it was that men like Chris - men who were handsome, smart, funny, sweet, reliable and trustworthy - came with a catch. As a result, I suffered from a certain level of anxiety about the relationship, which led to an ongoing quest to identify and break down the magic ingredient that made us work, and somehow that all translated into an obsession with milestones. It was as if the more milestones we could get through, the more tangible proof I'd have that we weren't too good to be true.

Since this was the longest relationship I'd ever had, technically every single day was a milestone. But when I explained this to Chris, he said "We're not celebrating each day we don't break up." So I was forced to find other milestones to celebrate, like the first time going to Chipotle, or our first time having lunch together on a week day, or starting our first Netflix series together. And he's great at playing along, but it's much easier for him to get excited about a legitimate milestone, like Meeting The Parents. Which is why while we were packing the car he'd periodically remind me that "THIS is a real milestone, babe!"

As we navigated the flooded roads and sheeting rain of Central Pennsylvania, Chris asked "So, how many people are going to be there tomorrow?"

"I think it's only going to be 12" I told him. Which was actually on the low side for a typical family gathering. Chris immediately started reciting everything he'd learned from studying Facebook. "Your sister Allison's husband's name is James, but you all call him Jim," he said with a slight sigh, as if we were purposely trying to trip him up with the nickname. "And your brother Jeremy is the one with all the little girls..."

"You know," I interrupted, in an effort to reduce his anxiety, "it's not like I need their approval in order to keep dating you." This was almost completely true, but it was a moot point because: a) one thing I knew for sure was that everyone ALWAYS likes Chris and b) I was 35 years old bringing home my first serious boyfriend. I knew my family would embrace anyone short of an escaped convict. And even then I think my dad would at least hear us out.

What I was really scared of was that Chris wasn't going to like my family. I love my family, and if he didn't, that could be a problem. This was one of *those* milestones, the kind that could change us. Unlike our first trip to Wegmans, for example.

Mostly I worried that Chris would find my family too overwhelming and chaotic. I'm one of 6 kids, and with almost everyone married with kids, chaotic and overwhelming is where we start. Chris and his one brother were raised by their single mother. From what I'd seen so far, his holidays and family gatherings were quiet, orderly affairs, even with his two teenage daughters. My biggest fear was that at the end of the weekend he'd say "Phew! Let's not do that very often."

The night we arrived we had dinner alone with my parents and, as I'd expected, it went very smoothly and Chris and my parents were fast friends.

The next morning as we waited in the kitchen of my parents' one bedroom condo for everyone else to arrive, Chris was definitely a little nervous, but I think I was more nervous. "If my brothers try to play the protective role and use words like intentions, just walk away," I told him.

Chris looked at me sideways before saying, "I'm not going to do that." So I just prayed silently that my sisters would refrain from using words like "weddings" or "babies" or "sebatious cysts" - one of my sisters can be gross at times.

As everyone piled into the condo, Chris and I quickly lost each other in the crowded space. We barely interacted beyond occasional eye contact until we sat down to eat. "How's it going?" I whispered. "Are you ok?"

"Don't worry about me, you just enjoy your time with your family," he said with a pat on my knee and I wondered if the unspoken was "because we're never doing this again."

Despite how well things had been going I was expecting dinner to change all of that. My family loves it when new people visit because it lets us show off how weird and hilarious (we believe) we are. Everyone is a little bolder and a little funnier when operating as a group, so "pass the bread" means a quarterback pass the length of the table, and the simplest comment is an invitation to a battle of the wits. I'd always loved my role in these games, but of course, I'd never been the one bringing in the new person. I flashed back to my role in hazing my sister's boyfriends, and my whole body tensed as I waited for their retribution.

But aside from when my 92 year old grandma gave me a thumbs up and said, at full volume in her Bronx accented trill, "Meredith, he's very cute. Well done!" nothing particularly embarrassing happened. No food was thrown, no one used the word poop inappropriately, and even my anti-social autistic nephew tried to engage Chris in conversation by asking him about video games.

All along I'd been so focused on what this milestone meant for me and Chris, I'd never considered that this was a milestone for my family too. They didn't know what the magic ingredient was between me and Chris any more than I did, but more to the point, they didn't know why I'd waited so long to bring someone home, and nobody wanted to be the one who said or did the thing to ruin it all.

I also like to believe that they were thinking "This is a great relationship; let's support it" rather than "if this doesn't work, she'll bring home 12 cats next time!" But either way, I'll take it.

The next morning my parents walked us out to the car and hugs were exchanged all the way around. As we backed out of the driveway Chris shook his head and said, "Your parents are so cute. And your family's really fun. I hope our next visit is longer." And I let out the breath I'd been holding for weeks. And when we went up for Thanksgiving, we stayed an extra day.

And then something completely unexpected happened. I stopped obsessing over milestones. In fact, I totally forgot to acknowledge our 11 month anniversary or our first snowfall. And when we hit our one year anniversary, I realized that maybe, just maybe, the magic ingredient was simply, love.

The Dream of the Cuttlefish
By Jeffrey Brady

Sloshing around the shallows of Micronesia swims a creature unlike any other in the sea.

The cuttlefish is a cephalopod and cousin to the squid. But unlike its relative, it has an epidermis filled with colored cells, like television pixels. With these, it can mimic, chameleon-like, the surrounding seabed.

His kiss tasted of the ocean. Or possibly McDonald's fries, from where he worked... Whichever, it was delicious. My hands were half-way down Michael's shirt, diving into his chest of blond hair. He cocked his head back. I inhaled the salty scent of his neck. That's when I heard the jingle of keys, the predatory thump of boots on the cypress wood dock. It was almost midnight. We sat, feet dangling above the bayou. Someone was coming. Two silhouettes approached. Beyond the trees, I saw the distant flicker of a patrol car.

"Son, wacchu, uh -- two... um... boys -- doin' on this here dock?" Voice gruff, keys jangling, he trained the beam at me, then Michael.

The glare of flashlight revealed Michael's shirt unevenly buttoned. It flashed briefly at our (thankfully) zippered jeans. Summer cicadas shrieked.

"Um, officer, we were just talking – I, I thought this

was a public dock!"

"Nah, son, this here's private property -- closed at sunset! Y'all best move along and stop loitering." He slapped at a mosquito. "You don't belong here!"

Like most people in Louisiana, this cop wasn't exactly homophobic. He simply couldn't comprehend the whole gay thing. Like gumbo without shrimp -- it just didn't make sense to him.

When in danger, the cuttlefish can impersonate a craggy rock, a wispy tendril of kelp, a sandy seabed. It moves stealthily, syncing its markings to the shimmering sunlight, the rhythm of waves. Its locomotion is speedy, literally jet-propelled.

Long associated with literature, it has a special place in the ancient world: the Romans sourced sepia from the creature. It siphons out ink when scared.

The officer was right... I didn't really belong there. Sure, I had family, festivals and food in Louisiana... but surviving required constant vigilance, wrapping myself in camouflage-feigned football fandom (Geaux, Tigers!).

So, I reached out: applying for jobs in DC. My K Street internship the previous winter had been exciting. I'd adored my unpaid nonprofit work, met fascinating people (handshake sharking like a Hill staffer), and never once felt judged for being gay.

I cast a wide net, searching for jobs and even posting an

online personal ad. Instead of the clichéd "long walks on the beach" approach, I posted an essay. It was a thought experiment that was the exact opposite of the usual personal ad: vague, abstract and quirky. It sounded like a National Geographic article. "The dream of the cuttlefish," I titled it, borrowing from a speech I heard in college. The talk involved the future of online interaction: the way we will all get along within the next 50 years. I used the speech as a springboard, diving into the deep end by exploring the life of the cuttlefish. That alone I used as the text of the personal ad.

I got bites quickly, for both job applications and to the personal advert. By far, the best response, professional or personal was this: "Jeffrey, I've never even heard about the cuttlefish until today. But now, I want to learn everything there is to know about it," one responder, Steven, enthused. A sweet idealist at an education nonprofit, he was also a dancer. The first time I heard his voice, as reedy as a band room oboe, I felt as if I were floating in an ocean on a golden afternoon. It was effortless and transformative. I couldn't remember the last time I felt so easily understood by another person. (Had I ever?) We talked on the phone for weeks. A job interview for a DC area university gave me the chance with a paid plane ticket and hotel stay to meet Steven.

September 11, 2001. Stormy, murky waters. My interview was postponed. Steven and I stared up at silent skies and discussed all that has happened to our country.

The cuttlefish recreates the colors of its environment as it hunts for its prey: little crabs and other mollusks. Of course, being a soft-bodied creature it's defenseless against the sharp pincers of its food source. Approaching with arms open wide, it exposes its vulnerable side, where its mouth is located, facing the opponent. The cuttlefish attacks, consuming its prey. You have to pity the little crab. Just before being stung, it is wrapped up in a singular, eight-limbed embrace that was, essentially, invisible, just a split-second before.

This full-body color morphing isn't solely used in hunting. The cuttlefish also uses it to communicate intention, even to attract a mate. Pfeffer's Flamboyant Cuttlefish (possibly the gayest scientific nomenclature ever) is particularly stunning.

Flights resumed, returning us to an uneasy calm. I breathed in the recycled air at 30,000 feet, animating Steven's picture matching his voice. Cardigan clad university officials met me at Dulles Airport, driving me back to a motel. The car-ride exchange went OK, but I was sweating it in an ill-chosen wool blazer. A maelstrom of half-truths pour forth from my lips: "Yes, I am excited about the position!" "No, I'm not nervous about the interview and faculty presentation!"

I find myself in a dank motel room, just beyond the beltway's whooshing surf of white noise. Bathroom cigarette burns and a sticky light switch cast suspicions about the bedding. Steven arrives with a "shave and a haircut, two bits" knock at the door. Waltzing in, he is all smiling dimples. We sit at the tiny lop-sided table. Pleasantries exchanged, the conversation quickly percolates with jokes, silly impressions and ridiculous chemistry. His hair is golden and I am mesmerized by how it glows in the dim light cast by the crooked lamp. Atop the crown of his head, I notice his perfect swirl of hair. I had to fight to keep my finger from tracing it.

We're halfway through an order of cheese biscuits at a nearby seafood joint before I realized that we are holding both hands on top of the table, in a public restaurant, and nobody cares. Not a single glance, not a ripple! Better yet, our conversation flows effortlessly. Nothing forced.

"What kind of job is this, anyway?" He wants to know. I want to confess that the job was not my main objective here. "Well, I can't really discuss it right now, I am on a more important mission, but I promise to tell you all about it one day" I demure, winking at him. Sipping my ice tea, I wonder if he can hear how fast my heart is beating.

He is an athletic conversationalist. Not content in the shallows, he plunges like a cliff diver. So animated. I stare at Steven's sturdy hands, full lips and arching eyebrows. We discuss our passions, hinting at new ones.

Internally, the cuttlefish has a unique physiology. Distinct from its squid relatives, it has a structure called a cuttlebone. It provides the animal with the means to regulate its gas-to-liquid ratio, thus the power to regulate its buoyancy. What must that feel like? To rise and fall, according to whim?

We are back in the dim room. Steven shimmers, a light

source in his own right, beneath water-stained prints of lighthouses. We kiss. I am floating. It is a full-body, activate all pleasure centers of the brain, swimming in his lips, experience. A Homeric Epic. We explore the suspicious bedding. Any thought of my job prospect has vanished. After what seems like a few minutes, it is dawn.

Morning light pokes through broken window blinds. We interlace fingers, whisper promises and linger in a languorous goodbye hug. My ride to the interview will arrive in any second. Steven's scruff, combined with his vigorous kissing, has left my face chapped and raw.

During the two-hour interview, I am floundering, distracted by the previous 10 hours of bliss. I ramble through some questions, stumblingly half-answer others and sink into a morass of missing the point. The presentation goes worse, running aground completely. "Ladies and gentlemen, thank you for your time and attention. Any questions?" I half expect someone to counter, "Was your face attacked by a school of raging jellyfish?" It is a Bermuda Triangle of furrowed brows, confused glares and face-palms. Through waiting room glass window blinds, I see the head of the interview committee. He yanks off his tie, folds his arms and gestures in my general direction. Soon, I decipher his shadow play display: The ride back to the airport, traditionally given by the head of the interview panel, is made slightly more awkward by the fact that the he patently refuses to take me. A taxi is called. Needless to say, I was not offered the job.

Back to Louisiana, Steven and I fall into a rhythm. We are on the phone for hours, speaking in the superlatives of teenagers, steady as the tide. By November, he has invited me to stay at his place, to aide the job search. I accept without a pause.

The blood of the animal is an unusual green-blue. It is pumped rapidly. The cuttlefish does not have a big heart. It has three.

Scientists speculate that the eyes of the cephalopod are fully formed before birth – that they observe their surroundings while still forming in the egg. They know what they want, from very early on. Unlike mammalian eyes, the cuttlefish has no blind spot.

Steven is a gracious and generous host. He spends hours showing me the sights of Washington, DC. I love the FDR Memorial by moonlight, ice sparkling in the fountains. We strolled, holding our mitten-clad hands. Whipping out a camera, we snapped pictures of each other queuing up among statues of breadlines, exaggerating pouts of the dispossessed. We explored the National Zoo, crunching leaves underfoot as the pandas gnaw on bamboo. In sync with their moving mouths, we interject silly dialog. "Butterstick, you need to sneeze in a ridiculously cute manner so we can make a hit YouTube video. We need media buzz!" Giggling at our improvisation, we rub noses. The pandas defecate adorably.

Going to performances with Steven is a real thrill for me. At his dance recitals, his leaps reveal him to be a creature of the air: angelic and graceful. He lights up the stage. Afterward, I revel in the cast wrap-parties. He pulls me through crowded English basement apartments, glancing back with a smile and a wink, twisting us through groves of broad-shouldered dancers. I get a particular rush from this simple act of kindness. My stomach leaps, too, every time he introduces me as his "boyfriend." His fellow dancers light up and enthuse, "Oh, so you're the one! We've heard so much about you."

Even with all the fun, Steven also scares me sometimes. He demonstrates a habit of running red lights that simultaneously baffles and terrifies. In his giant SUV, Steven must have felt invulnerable, I suppose. Lead-footing the gas pedal, he sped through red lights with a peculiar jocularity, punctuating the act by kissing his hand, then tapping the ceiling of the cab. These brushes with chance left me unsettled but unscathed. Eventually, I got used to them, even while I clutched the driver's side handle, white-knuckled.

I remain at his apartment until January, when I finally get a job.

There are fewer invitations to dance recitals. There is a slight change in the air between us. He tells me on the Metro train. We had been holding hands when he pulls back, retreats within himself. "Jeffrey, listen. Thank you for these months together, but I don't love you anymore."

"Doors closing," chimed the train. I felt the emptiness inside my gloves, grasping at nothing, alone in a crowded train car, in the dark depths beneath DuPont

Circle. It seemed that whatever currents had brought us together could not last. We had drifted.

Imagine for a second that you could rearrange yourself like a cuttlefish: alter color, texture and form. Picture your internal dance fully realized for all to see. We are limited to very crude tools to describe and explain ourselves. Physical expressions, music, images and our words are all we have to convey our rich inner worlds.

As Flaubert reminds us, "Human speech is like a cracked kettle on which we tap crude rhythms for bears to dance to, while we long to make music that will melt the stars."

How intimate. How lovely. How human, to share ourselves, our inner stories made flesh.

Despite our breakup, I remain grateful to Steven. He gave me so much. He gave me a real reason to migrate to this area – much better than the abstract prospect of a job. He brought me to a new habitat, where I didn't need camouflage. He brought me to a place to shimmer, to thrive, to flourish. He brought me to a place where I could be myself.

The Flaw of Attraction
By Nevin Martell

When I was in my twenties, there was nothing I loved more than a flawed dating prospect. There was the cute actress who talked like she had been sucking on a helium tank; the fun loving party girl who liked to get really drunk and take her clothes off in public; the attractive marathoner who couldn't have sex without crying.

I'm sure they all found me intrinsically flawed in some way, too, depending on when they had the dubious honor of dating me. I had a mullet in junior high that Billy Ray Cyrus would have envied; in college I was prone to getting stoned and yelling, "I am the lizard king!" from the fire escape; as a so-called adult, I spent the better part of two years watching *Law and Order* reruns while collecting unemployment checks from the comfort of my foldup futon couch.

But for every rule there's an exception.

I went to high school with a girl named Indira, who everyone called Indie. We lived in the small town of Clinton, NY, but we were both transplants. She was born in Ghana in West Africa, while I had just moved back to the States after being in New Zealand for several years.

That made us both the kids in our classes who talked funny. She had a clipped African tone, while I said foreign sounding things with a Kiwi lilt, like "G'day mate, care to grab some Weet-Bix for brekkie?"

The first time I met Indie, I used that charming accent to scream at her, "Get the fuck out of my house!"

That's because she, my sister, and a few other friends were raiding my father's liquor cabinet while my parents were out of town. It wasn't that I was frowning on the potential negative health affects brought on by underage drinking or the immorality of their theft – I was simply afraid that I would be blamed and punished for their indiscretions.

It would be understandable if Indie left that encounter thinking that I was a little flawed.
I didn't see her again for more than a decade when we both found ourselves back in our hometown. I was at nearby Syracuse University for grad school, while she was taking care of her then ailing mother and working as a lawyer. We had been casually emailing for a couple of years, after we got reconnected through the social networking failure known as Friendster.com. She had a cute picture and her short emails were always witty, so I figured I would ask her out to lunch to cut the boredom of being at home.

When I showed up for our rendezvous, I was shocked. The last time I had seen her, she had been a scrappy little girl with braids, a love of Day-Glo plastic jewelry, and a bottle of my father's prized Glenlivet scotch clutched in her right hand. Now she was a woman – a really hot woman. She had big beautiful eyes, tight jeans, and a smile that could sell a billion tubes of Crest. I knew from our emails that she was very smart, since she had gone to law school and was in the midst of studying for the New York bar exam.

Naturally, I freaked out a little bit. This woman was way out of my league, and I knew it.

Miraculously, she didn't seem to know it. But how long could such severe oversight last? I decided my only shot was to try to keep her laughing so that she couldn't focus on my countless faults or spend the whole time thinking, "What the fuck was I thinking, agreeing to have lunch with this loser?"

My tactic worked well. She smiled a lot, laughed at all my jokes, and she didn't once bring up my mullet. About halfway through the meal, just after I told a joke that had gone over particularly well, I felt Indie's leg rub up against mine. I would have given myself a mental high five, except that there was one small problem: the rubbing wasn't particularly provocative. It was like a jackhammer gone rogue.

What should I do? If she was trying to be sexy, who was I to complain? If she had some health problem, I was going to look like a bastard if I made a big deal out of it. So I didn't say anything at first. By the end of the meal though, her leg was moving even faster, her heels leaving inch-deep indentations on the top of my throbbing left foot. I had to say something, because I didn't want to blurt out something insanely rude in a moment of pain, such as, "Get off my fucking foot, you crazy woman."

Instead, I opted for, "Excuse me, I don't think you're aware of this, but your foot is on my foot."

"It is?" she asked, blushing as she looked under the table where I was trying to delicately extricate my mangled limb. "This is really embarrassing. I bounce my leg when I'm nervous. I'm so, so sorry."

She was sorry? I was the sorry one. What an idiot I'd been to bring it up! I'd blown it, and now she'd never see me again. I'd just be some guy she had an awkward lunch with once. I knew I should probably just slink out the back door, but I couldn't, because the fucked up little Jiminy Cricket on my shoulder was telling me to ask her out again.

To my surprise, she not only agreed, but also joked, "Don't worry, I'll sit on the far side of the table next time."

That lunch turned into yet another one, which lacked a podiatric freak out. A few months later, we started dating. When my graduate program finished that summer, I moved down to D.C. Despite the long distance separating us, our relationship flourished. We played Internet Scrabble and chatted over the phone almost every night; we mailed each other care packages full of home baked goodies; and we made a point of getting together as often as we could.

Really early on in our relationship, I knew I was in way

over my head. Indie was not a flawed prospect by any gauge, especially compared to my earlier misfires. The very fact that she didn't like to get drunk and take her clothes off in bars put her way above the competition. I quickly realized that I was stupid in love and I was trying to figure out how to express that. Since there's no better time to show how smitten you are than on Valentine's Day, I decided to go all out for Cupid's favorite holiday.

When February 14 rolled around, we exchanged gifts. Indie went first, and gave me a t-shirt that I can't wear in public because it makes me feel neutered. (It has Voltron on it and says, "You complete me." It would have been cool if it had it just been the robot, but the *Jerry McGuire* reference was a deal breaker.)

I may have gone a little overboard with my present. For a week, I ran around D.C. like a love struck fool with a sign proclaiming my unabashed love for Indie. It read, I (Heart) I.O. (the initials stood for Indira Odamtten). While friends videotaped me and tried not to laugh too hard, I danced with my little billboard in front of famous landmarks and places that meant a lot to us personally, such as 2 Amys Pizza, which she had gotten me hooked on. I took all this footage and edited it to our song, "With Arms Outstretched" by Rilo Kiley. The resulting music video was my Valentine's Day gift.

It was a huge hit. She loved it. Even her parents were impressed when she showed it to them. Suddenly, I wasn't just the guy who was dating their daughter; I was the guy who was in love with their daughter.

A couple years later, I knew I was ready to take the next step in our relationship, but I didn't know how I was going to get her to say yes to me. I thought I had to do something really, really big – even bigger than an MTV-worthy music video. For days, I mulled my romantic conundrum until I finally had an epiphany: I would make a movie preview of our future life together.

I would take her to dinner, and then on to a movie theatre, which I would have rented out and filled with paid extras posing as moviegoers. The lights would go down and then the gravitas-filled voiceover guy would begin, "In a world of darkness...torn asunder by chaos and evil...two soul mates found each other...and became one of the greatest love stories ever told."

This would be accompanied by a montage of shots – us dressed up all fancy for our first big date, playing beer pong at a grad school party, and summer vacation on Cape Cod – while epic music from *Legends of the Fall* swelled up dramatically. It was going to be the most amazing preview, ever. I wanted it to be so good that other people in the theatre would be compelled to propose to the person sitting next to them, even if they didn't know each other.

Then came the inevitable self-immolating meltdown when I realized that I was going way overboard. I recognized movie preview proposal wasn't about us anymore; it was about me doing something big and over-the-top that one-upped myself.

Indie needed to say, "Yes, I do want to spend my life with you, you crazy boy," because she wanted to marry **me**, not the spectacle.

So, I dialed it way back, nixing the preview entirely. Instead, the proposal went down at my childhood home on the afternoon of Christmas Eve in front of a roaring fire. It was just the two of us. There wasn't any epic music, there was no montage, and the only scripted line was, "Will you marry me?"

She said, "Yes."

Authors Note: This story was originally performed live on my first Valentine's Day as a married man. I had been trying to figure out how my declaration of love for Indie could top a music video, a marriage proposal, and a wedding. She thought I was performing a completely different story when I got up on stage that night. Telling a room full of strangers how I fell in love with her seemed like the only logical route to take to outdo myself. What else could I do after that, except include that story in this anthology?

The Elephant Graveyard
By Vijai Nathan

Two things you should know about me: I'm Indian and I suck at dating.

I was raised to get an arranged marriage and until that day I was to have no contact with the opposite sex— my father was very clear: "Vijai, men are animals. You go near them, they go crazy, and they rape you. You look at them, they rape you. You make them a cheese sandwich, they rape you."

I followed his advice my whole life and now... I am pissed because my parents did not come through with my arranged marriage. I missed out on years of figuring out the opposite sex and I am left with none of the dating tools that most girls in America grow up learning.

I'm totally clueless when it comes to reading a potentially "sexual" situation or figuring out if a guy is hitting on me. I was on a business trip about 5 years ago, when my co-worker invited me to have a drink with him in his hotel room. We're just sitting on his bed, chatting about music and he says "What would you do if I pulled out my dick right now?"

"Um—weren't we just talking about Fleetwood Mac? How did we get from the hauntingly beautify voice of Stevie Nicks to your dick? Umm, I'm not sure what I would do, but I would definitely not make you a cheese sandwich...."

I am still single and ALL my friends say "Go online, there are sooo many nice guys online!"

And I'm thinking, "Have they seen NBC's To Catch a Predator? NO thanks."

But it was my mom's encouraging words: "Vijai please do something—your eggs are rotting every day. Last year your egg could have been a doctor. This year a pizza guy. Next year a Republican...."

I half-heartedly join some dating sites-- both Indian and American ones, and there are big differences. For instance, "Turn-Ons"-- On match.com it's all "Long Hair, Sense of Humor, Brainiacs." On Indian dating.com the turn-ons are "American Citizenship."

One day, I find myself sitting at home alone on a Friday night, crying and drinking a box of chardonnay, while watching that scrappy Meg Ryan on You've Got Mail when I decide to join.....E-harmony.

The act of joining this site to me is comparable to the idea of "The Elephant Graveyard." Out in the jungle, when an elephant knows he is going to die, his body moves to his final resting place. E-harmony is the elephant graveyard of online dating—it is where ugly people go to die.

I spend the next three hours answering 500 questions and I wait for that creepy white dude, Dr. Kevorkian, or Warren, or whatever his name is, to send my matches.

Minutes later, my "man buffet" magically arrives and I'm ready to dig in! I'm going through them, one by one, and it is looking bleak. I am trying to figure out to which question I answered "Yes! I will date every member of a Dungeons & Dragons Fan Club." These guys were the ripe combination of both hideous and weird... They were "one-turkey-leg-away-from-the-Renaissance-Fair" kind of weird.

And I am not a shallow person, I will date conventionally ugly people- like Tom Arnold, Don Knots, Gerard Depardieu. But the guys on this site were the top contenders in a Gollum Look-a-Like contest.

At this point I am just trying to pick the least bruised banana in the bunch, and I find one guy who looks decent. He's not smiling in any of his pictures, but it gives him a sexy brooding quality and I start to think, "This a complex man—I can do a complex man—like Heathcliff in *Wuthering Heights*, or Mr. Darcy in *Pride and Prejudice*, or Richard Gere in *Pretty Woman.*

We meet for a drink and I am so happy, because he looks exactly like his picture. I smile and say hi, and he smiles..... and I immediately see why he did not have any pictures of him smiling in his profile.

This guy has the most jacked up teeth I have ever seen in my life.

It was like looking into a cavern, with stalactites and stalagmites. I didn't know where his teeth ended or began. And his mouth was huge- like a T-Rex, but a T-Rex on Chrystal Meth. This man could have been the love child of a caveman and anyone British.

All I keep thinking is that E-harmony is expensive... he should use the money for a new set of teeth.

Then it hits me. I am the hot one, the Pamela Anderson, in this scenario. And I love it, because I am NEVER the hot one. In my hotness, I am suddenly feeling benevolent and I decide to do a solid to this dentally-challenged gentleman, because I sense that I am the closest this man has been to a vagina since his actual birth.

I decide that I am going to be nice, I am going to be the Mother Teresa of dating and give him the best date he has ever had in his life—I am even going to ignore my pre-planned fake emergency phone call from my sister.

So I pump up the charm and sparkle, push out my boobs and things are going great. Then his cell rings and he says "Hi. Oh Dude—are you okay? I'll be right there."

"Is everything okay?"

"Gosh, I gotta go, my brother is locked outside of his apartment."

"Oh. Oh?!" Wait a second—this guy is trying to pull a

fake emergency on me?! What the fuck? I'm the hot one—and he's the jacked-up T-Rex. What was he going to do? Rush home to watch a Battlestar Galactica marathon?

I am pissed, so I say, "First of all, Dude, I know exactly what you are doing. Second- that is the lamest "emergency" I have ever heard in my life. So you just sit right here, because in two minutes, my sister is going to call, and she's going to be lying in a ditch, bleeding by the side of the road, just outside a prison, where a man with a hook for an arm is on the loose. Now that is an emergency."

After that, I kept clear of men for a while. My dad was right, men are animals. And I decided to never go on another online date again.... unless I can see his teeth in the photo.

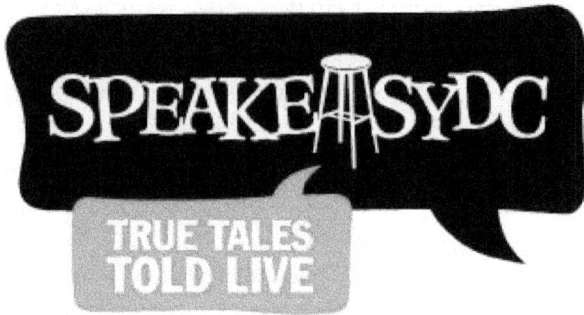

SpeakeasyDC's mission is to present contemporary autobiographical story performance at its best, to grow the number of storytelling artists and fans in the region from a wide-range of communities, and to strengthen SpeakeasyDC's role as the nation's go-to place for training in the art of storytelling. At its best, this kind of storytelling is both entertaining and thought-provoking, and captures a diverse set of life experiences.

We believe that this uniquely personal exchange enriches our understanding of the self and the "other" and promotes curiosity, compassion, and connection. We strive to elevate the craft of storytelling through our classes and coaching; nurture and support new artists; and create a safe and welcoming environment for diverse perspectives."

Find out more at www.speakeasydc.org

www.ingramcontent.com/pod-product-compliance
Lightning Source LLC
Chambersburg PA
CBHW060701030426
42337CB00017B/2708